TAMILNADU HOSPITAL REPORTER

Dr.K.Murugesan,MBBS,AFIH.,

Dr. K. MURUGESAN , MBBS,AFIH.,

ISBN: 1731515103

ISBN-13: 9781731515100

DEDICATION

I dedicate this book for those doctors, Nurses and All Healthcare Staffs who work hard to save patient's lives .

Dr. K. MURUGESAN , MBBS,AFIH.,

CONTENTS

Dr. K. MURUGESAN , MBBS,AFIH.,

ACKNOWLEDGMENTS

This book is an effort to make a directory of hospitals in Tamilnadu to help people to know the nearest hospital from there house when they are in need of medical treatment in case of medical emergency and for general health checkup . The hospital names listed in this book are for information purpose only .We do not recommend any hospitals for treatment . Your family doctor will be a better advisor for choosing best hospital depending upon the severity of disease . The list provided in this book is not a complete list .We will update missed hospitals in our future editions to make this book a complete directory .

1 CHENNAI

Apollo Children's Hospitals
Address: No. 15, Shafee Mohammed Rd, Thousand Lights West, Thousand Lights, Chennai, Tamil Nadu 600006
Phone : 044 2829 8282

Apollo Hospitals
Address: No: 21, Greams Lane, Off Greams Road, Chennai, Tamil Nadu 600006
Phone : 044 2829 0200

Apollo Speciality Hospitals
Address : 5/639, Old Mahabalipuram Road, Perungudi, Chennai, Tamil Nadu 600096

Dr. K. MURUGESAN , MBBS,AFIH.,

Phone : 044 3322 1111

Apollo Speciality Hospitals

Address: Plot No 64, Vanagaram-Ambattur Rd,
Ayanambakkam, Kil Ayanambakkam, Chennai, Tamil
Nadu 600095
 Phone: 044 2653 7777

Apollo Cancer Institutes

Address: Anna Salai, Rathna Nagar, Alwarpet,
Chennai, Tamil Nadu 600035

Appasamy Hospitals

Address: No. 1 and 2, SBI Officers Colony, 1st Street,
Near Chennai Ford, Arumbakkam, Chennai, Tamil
Nadu 600106
Phone: 044 3059 5979

Billroth Hospital

Address: 43, Lakshmi Talkies Road, Shenoy Nagar,
Chennai, Tamil Nadu 600030
Phone: 044 4292 1777

Dr. Mehta's Hospitals

Address: No.2, Mc Nichols Rd, Chetpet, Chennai,
Tamil Nadu 600031

Phone: 044 4227 1001

Fortis Malar Hospital
Address: No. 52, 1st Main Rd, Gandhi Nagar, Adyar, Chennai, Tamil Nadu 600020
Phone: 099625 99933

Gosha Hospital
Address: 105, Bells Rd, Police Quarters, Triplicane, Chennai, Tamil Nadu 600005

Madras Institute of Orthopaedics and Traumatology
Address: 4/112, Mount Poonamalle High Rd, Sathya Nagar, Manapakkam, Chennai, Tamil Nadu 600089
Phone: 044 4200 2288

Parvathy Hospital
Address: 241, GST Road Chromepet, Near MIT Bridge, Chennai, Tamil Nadu 600044
Phone: 044 2238 2248

Rainbow Children's Hospital
157, Anna Salai, Near Little Mount Metro Station, Guindy, Chennai 600015
044 40122444

SIMS Hospital

Address: (Next to Vadapalani Metro Station) No.1, Jawaharlal Nehru Salai(100 Feet Road), Vadapalani, Chennai, Tamil Nadu 600026
Phone: 044 4921 1455

Venkataeswara Hospitals

Address: 36 - A, Pasumpon Muthuramalinga Thevar Road, Nandanam Extension, Nandanam, Chennai, Tamil Nadu 600035
Phone: 044 4511 1111

Vijaya Hospital

Address: 434, PT Rajan Rd, N.S.K, Vadapalani, Chennai, Tamil Nadu 600026
Phone: 044 6664 6600

VS Hospitals

Address: #13, E Spur Tank Rd, Chetpet, Chennai, Tamil Nadu 600031
Phone: 044 4200 1000

2 .THIRUVALLUR

CSI Hospital

Address: Tiruvallur, Tamil Nadu 602001
Phone: 044 2766 5981

Goverment Hospital

Address: SH 57, Hariram Nagar, Poonga Nagar,
Kakkalur, Tamil Nadu 602001

G.K. Hospital

Address: No: 4, Navalar Street, Near Venkateswara
Theatre, Manavalanagar, Tiruvallur, Tamil Nadu
602002
Phone: 044 2764 2202

Janani Hospital

Address: No.5, JN Rd, MGM Nagar, Tiruvallur, Tamil
Nadu 602001
Phone: 044 2766 6668

Mj orthocare hospital

Address: No. 36, Jain Nagar, Opp Vasan Eye Care
Hospital, Jain Road, district, Tiruvallur, 602001
Phone: 044 2766 0265

RKB Hospitals

Address: RKB Hospitals, 45, JN Rd, Rajajipuram,
Periyakuppam, Tiruvallur, Tamil Nadu 602001
Phone: 044 2766 0479

SM Hospital
Address: MSR Complex, 4/120, Thiruvallur, SH-57,
Tiruvallur Uthukottai Road, Thiruvallur, Tiruvallur,
602001
Phone: 08508286163

Dr. K. MURUGESAN , MBBS,AFIH.,

3 . KANCHIPURAM

ABCD Hospitals

Address: No.14, Ulagalandha Perumal Koil Sannadhi Street, Near Sri Kanchi Kamakshi Amman Temple, Kanchipuram, Tamil Nadu 631501
Phone: 044 2723 2074

C S I Hospital

Address: Hospital Road, Ennaikaran, Kanchipuram, Tamil Nadu 631501
Phone: 044 2723 1867

EMMESS Women Care Centre
Address: Hospital Rd, Nellukara st, Kanchipuram,
Tamil Nadu 631502
Phone: 096293 53513

Govt. District Head Quarters Hospital
Address: Hospital Road, Ennaikaran, Kanchipuram,
Tamil Nadu 631501

Life Care Hospital
Address: 15, Railway Rd, Min Nagar, Kanchipuram,
Tamil Nadu 631501
Phone: 044 2723 1090

Lakshmi Hospital
Address: Plot No.46, Nellukara Street, Beside Kalyan
Jewellers, Kanchipuram, Tamil Nadu 631501
Phone: 044 2722 3903

Manohar General Hospital

Address: 28, Railway Rd, Min Nagar, Kanchipuram,
Tamil Nadu 631501
Phone: 044 6727 6777

Narbhavi Hospital

Address: 55A, SVN Pillai St, Pillaiyarpalayam,
Kanchipuram, Tamil Nadu 631502
Phone: 074483 74483

Meenakshi Medical College Hospital And Research Institute

Address: Enathur, Karrapettai Post, Kanchipuram,
Tamil Nadu 631552
Phone: 044 2726 1337

Orthocare Physiotherapy Hospital

Address: 100/77, Nethaji Nagar, Kanchipuram, SH-58,
Kanchipuram Chengalpattu Road, Kanchipuram,
Kanchipuram, 631501
Phone: 044 2722 2280

Sri Ne Medical Foundation
Address: No. 53, M M Ave 1st Main Rd, Ennaikaran,
Kanchipuram, Tamil Nadu 631501
Phone: 044 2722 8614

Sri D.K.K Hospital
Address: Nadu St, Ennaikaran, Kanchipuram, Tamil
Nadu 631501
Hours:
Open 24 hours
Phone: 086681 02429

VKJ Hospital
Address: 8A, Nellukara St, Ennaikaran, Kanchipuram,
Tamil Nadu 631502
Phone: 044 2723 5599

4 .VELLORE

Christian Medical College
Address: Arni RoadBagayam, Thorapadi, Vellore,
Tamil Nadu 632002
Phone: 0416 228 4255

Dinesh Hospital
Address: 24/B, Arni Road, Vellore, Tamil Nadu
632001
Phone: 0416 222 3300

Dr Sivakumar Multi Speciality Hospital
Address: C-3, Phase-II, Opp to Collector Office, Arcot
Road, Sathuvachari, Vellore, Tamil Nadu 632009
Phone: 0416 225 2114

Indira Nursing Home
Address: No 452, Main Bazaar Road, Saidapet, Near
CMC, Vellore, Tamil Nadu 632012

Kumaran Hospital
Address: 112, Katpadi Road, Gandhinagar, Near
Kotak Mahindra Bank, Vellore, Tamil Nadu 632006
Phone: 0416 224 3630

Manisundaram Medical Mission Hospital
Address: 288, Phase – 1, Near More Supermarket,
South Avenue Road Vallalar, Vellore, Tamil Nadu
632009
Phone: 0416 225 4007

Dr. K. MURUGESAN , MBBS,AFIH.,

Sandhya Hospital
Address: No.565,, Phase.I, Sathuvachary, Vellore,
Tamil Nadu 632009
Phone: 0416 225 3357

Sri Narayani Hospital & Research Centre
Address: Azad Road, Sripuram, Thirumalaikodi,
Vellore, Tamil Nadu 632055
Phone: 0416 220 6300

5. THIRUVANNAMALAI

Grace and compassion Hospital
Address: No. 57, Thindivanam Road, Anna salai,
Tiruvannamalai, Tamil Nadu 606601
Phone: 04175 254 463

Government Tiruvannamalai Medical College and Hospital
Address: Outer Ring Road New town, Thirinjapuram
Union, Vengikkal, Tiruvannamalai, Tamil Nadu
606604

Dr. K. MURUGESAN , MBBS,AFIH.,

Phone: 04175 233 315

Raj Hospital

Address: 24 Hours Emergency Hospital In
Thiruvannamalai No.10/7c,Mannu pillai Nagar, Pey
Gopuram 1st Street, Chengam Road, Tiruvannamalai,
Tamil Nadu 606601
Phone: 097866 63744

SS Hospital

Address: 19, Mathalangulam St, Mathalangulam,
Tiruvannamalai, Tamil Nadu 606601
Phone: 04175 254 470

Star Hospital

Address: 34/64, Durgai Amman Koil St,
Mathalangulam, Tiruvannamalai, Tamil Nadu 606601
Phone: 04175 224 079

6. KRISHNAGIRI

ARK MULTISPECIALITY HOSPITAL
Address: 4th Cross Rd, Co-operative Colony,
Thiruvalluvar Nagar, Krishnagiri, Tamil Nadu 635001
Hours:
Open 24 hours
Phone: 04343 233 000

Government Hospital
Address: 43, Gandhi Road, Poonthottam, Veerappa
Nagar, Krishnagiri, Tamil Nadu 635001
Hours:

Dr. K. MURUGESAN , MBBS,AFIH.,

Open 24 hours
Phone: 04343 232 802

TCR MULTISPECIALITY HOSPITAL
Address: TCR MULTISPECIALITY HOSPITAL 1/450,
Avvai Nagar, Near TCR Circle, Chennai Bye-pass
Road, Krishnagiri, Tamil Nadu 635001
Hours:
Open 24 hours
Phone: 04343 239 393

7. DHARMAPURI

AP Hospital

Address: Nethaji Bypass Rd, Dharmapuri, Tamil Nadu
636701
Phone: 04342 260 139

Dr. K. MURUGESAN , MBBS,AFIH.,

BGR HOSPITAL

Address: Dharmapuri, Tamil Nadu 636701

Phone: 04342 267 177

Kamalam Hospital

Address: 248/53-M, Nethaji Bypass Road,

Dharmapuri, Tamil Nadu 636701

Phone: 04342 260 707

KV HOSPITAL

Address: No: 107, Nethaji Bypass, Near Malabar

Finance, Dharmapuri, Tamil Nadu 636701

Nithya Hospital

Address: Dharmapuri,, Indhira Nagar, Dharmapuri,

Tamil Nadu 636701

Phone: 04342 260 371

R.K. Hospital

Address: Nethaji Bypass, Dharmapuri, Tamil Nadu
636701
Phone: 04342 260 190

Supa Hospital

Address: CK Srinivasa Rao St, Dharmapuri, Tamil
Nadu 636701

8. VILUPPURAM

Aswini Hospital
Address: NH45A, Thiru Vi Ka Street, Villupuram,
Tamil Nadu 605602

Anand Hospital
Address: Trichy Trunck Rd, Moovendar Nagar,
Villupuram, Tamil Nadu 605602

Bharani Hospital

Address: Viluppuram, NH-45A, East Pondy Road,
Viluppuram, Villupuram, 605602
Phone: 04146 220 775

Devaki Hospital

Address: Chairman Chidam, K K Nagar, Villupuram,
Tamil Nadu 605602
Phone: 04146 251 023

Dr S Karthik Bhandary Hospital

Address: Viluppuram, NH-45A, East Pondy Road,
Viluppuram, Villupuram, 605602
Phone: 04146 222 009

Dr.P.D.R. Memorial hospital

Address: Chairman Chidam, K K Nagar, Villupuram,
Tamil Nadu 605602

Dr. K. MURUGESAN , MBBS,AFIH.,

Phone: 099436 40011

Durai Gastro Care

Address: Narayanan Nagar Road, Highways Nagar, K
K Nagar, Puntottam, Tamil Nadu 605602
Phone: 091513 12111

ES Hospital

Address: No: 32-B, Trichy Trunk Road, Villupuram,
Tamil Nadu 605602
Phone: 04146 251 035

Hari Hospital

Address: Viluppuram, NH-45A, East Pondy Road,
Viluppuram, Villupuram, 605602
Phone: 04146 259 574

Jai Sankara Hindu Mission Hospital

Address: No.11, Puntottam Pathai, Villupuram, Tamil
Nadu 605602

Phone: 04146 225 922

Koti Bone & Joint Ortho Hospital

Address: Chairman Chidam, K K Nagar, Villupuram,
Tamil Nadu 605602
Phone: 04146 223 882

Malar Hospital

Address: Trichy Trunck Rd, Kamala Nagar,
Villupuram, Tamil Nadu 605602

Maragadham Hospital

Address: E Pondy Rd, Near Gandhi Statue,
Mandhakarai, Villupuram, Tamil Nadu 605602
Phone: 04146 225 456

Royal Hospital

Address: Trichy Trunck Rd, K K Nagar, Villupuram,
Tamil Nadu 605602

Dr. K. MURUGESAN , MBBS,AFIH.,

Phone: 04146 221 118

Sumathi Nursing Home
Address: Nehruji Rd, Chairman Chidam, K K Nagar,
Villupuram, Tamil Nadu 605602
Phone: 04146 228 700

Shivam Multispeciality Hospitals
Address: Selva Nagar, Villupuram, Tamil Nadu
605602
Phone: 04146 228 080

South Zone Ent Research Centre
Address: Moovendar Nagar, Villupuram, Tamil Nadu
605602
Phone: 04146 259 194

TSR Hospital
Address: Thiru Vi Ka Street, Villupuram, Tamil Nadu
605602

Phone: 04146 222 760

Vasantham Health Center
Address: Kubera St, Fathima Layout, Villupuram,
Tamil Nadu 605602

Dr. K. MURUGESAN , MBBS,AFIH.,

9.CADDALORE

Krishna Hospital
Address: 17-A, Hospital Road, Cuddalore, Tamil Nadu
607001
Phone: 04142 231 714

Maruthi Gastro Care Hospital

Address: No. 42-43, Sekar Nagar, Semmandalam,
Cuddalore, Tamil Nadu 607001
Phone: 04142 284 666

Kannan Hospital

Address: 17, Bashyam St, Allpettai, Manjakuppam,
Cuddalore, Tamil Nadu 607001
Phone: 04142 230 370

PR Hospital

Address: Government TB Hospital, Opo,
Manjakuppam, Cuddalore, Tamil Nadu 607001
Phone: 04142 231 147

Saravana Hospital

Dr. K. MURUGESAN , MBBS,AFIH.,

Address: 47, Gundusalai Road, Pondy Bye-pass,
Cuddalore, Tamil Nadu 607001
Phone: 04142 231 662

Sujatha Hospital

Address: 78, Nethaji Rd, North Venugopalapuram,
Allpettai, Manjakuppam, Cuddalore, Tamil Nadu
607001
Phone: 04142 230 422

Lakshmi Hospital

Address: 40, Bashyam St, Allpettai, Govindasamy
Nagar, Cuddalore, Tamil Nadu 607001
Phone: 04142 220 604

Valli Vilas Hospital

Address: No: 45/2, Bharathy Road, Near Adyar
Anandha Bhavan, Manjakuppam, Cuddalore, Tamil
Nadu 607001
Phone: 094433 26879

ARR Hospital

Address: 34 B, Rajambal Nagar, Opp Head Post
Office, Allpettai, Manjakuppam, Cuddalore, Tamil
Nadu 607001
Phone: 04142 231 108

Subha Anandham Medical Centre

Address: 11A/3, Hospital Rd, Vilvarayanatham,
Manjakuppam, Cuddalore, Tamil Nadu 607001
Phone: 04142 222 092

New Life Hospital

Address: Dharkan Sahib Street, Manjakuppam,
Sorkalpet,, Manjakuppam, Cuddalore, Tamil Nadu
607001
Phone: 04142 221 567

Deepam hospital

Dr. K. MURUGESAN , MBBS,AFIH.,

Address: Semmandalam, Cuddalore, Tamil Nadu
607001
Phone: 073732 21224

10.SALEM

P.K.S HOSPITAL

Address: No: 40, Ammapet Main Rd, Ammapet,
Salem, Tamil Nadu 636001

Phone: 094432 88943

DR.RAMU LIFE CARE HOSPITAL

Address: 49/20, 2nd Agraharam, First Agraharam,
Salem, Tamil Nadu 636001
Phone: 098947 91272

Kauvery Hospital

Address: 9/50, Trichy Main Rd, Opp.to Chandra
Mahal, M G R Nagar, Seelanaickenpatti, Salem, Tamil
Nadu 636201
Phone: 0427 246 5555

Global Medical Centre

Address: 10-3/5, Jagir Ammapalayam, NH7,
Mallamooppampatti, Salem, Tamil Nadu 636302
Phone: 0427 234 0260

Vidya Hospital

Dr. K. MURUGESAN , MBBS,AFIH.,

Address: No 103 C, Behind Gandhi Stadium, Tamil
Sangam Road, Sankar Nagar, Salem, 636007
Phone: 0427 406 7777

Bhavani Hospital

Address: 20, Raghavan St, Swarnapuri, Salem, Tamil
Nadu 636004
Phone: 0427 233 3699

Palaniyandi Hospital

Address: Ammapet, Salem, Tamil Nadu 636003
Phone: 0427 224 4500

Devi Hospital

Address: New Fairlands, Alagapuram Pudur, Salem,
Tamil Nadu 636016
Phone: 0427 244 5607

SPMM Hospital

Address: 29, Cuddalore Main Road, Ammapet,,
Salem, Tamil Nadu 636003
Phone: 0427 224 4500

Manipal Hospitals

Address: Dalmia Board, Salem - Bangalore Highway,
Salem, Tamil Nadu 636012
Phone: 0427 234 6600

St Mary's Hospital

Address: Arisipalayam Main Road, Arisipalayam,
Salem, Tamil Nadu 636009
Phone: 0427 235 2988

Sri Vasantham Hospital

Address: No. 52/1, Opposite D.S.P. Office, Linemedu,
Gugai, Salem, Tamil Nadu 636006
Phone: 0427 246 5119

Government Medical College and Hospital

Address: Gmkmch, Shevapet, Salem, Tamil Nadu
636001
Phone: 0427 221 0674

TVG Hospital

Address: Trichy Road, Karungalpatty, Gugai, Salem,
Tamil Nadu 636006
Phone: 0427 221 0282

Dr. K. MURUGESAN , MBBS,AFIH.,

11.NAMAKKAL

Thangam Hospital
Address: 54, Dr. Sankaran Road, Near BSNL Office, KK
Nagar, Namakkal, Tamil Nadu 637001
Phone: 04286 230 685

M.M. Hospital

Address: 6/288, Trichy Main Road, Namakkal, Tamil
Nadu 637001
Phone: 097866 50575

Maruthi Hospital

Address: 743/E, Salem Road, Namakkal, Tamil Nadu
637001

Latha Eye Hospital

Address: Natarajapuram, Kamaraj Nagar, Namakkal,
Tamil Nadu 637001
 Phone: 04286 234 545

CM Hospital

Address: 2, Mohanur - Namakkal Rd, Gandhi Nagar,
Namakkal, Tamil Nadu 637001
Phone: 04286 220 800

Dr. K. MURUGESAN , MBBS,AFIH.,

Deepthi Multispeciality Hospital

Address: 31-A Mohanur Road, Namakkal, Tamil Nadu 637001
 Phone: 04286 222 396

Bharathi Hospital

Address: 452/454, Salem Main Road, Near KMS Lodge, Namakkal, Tamil Nadu 637001

Maharaja Speciality Hospital

Address: 78-C, Mohanur Rd, K K Nagar, Namakkal, Tamil Nadu 637001
Phone: 04286 234 620

Government Head Quarters Hospital

Address: Mohanur Road, Thillaipuram, Namakkal, Tamil Nadu 637001
Phone: 04286 221 203

R.K. Hospital

Address: 11A,Mohanur Road, Opposite to South School, Namakkal, Tamil Nadu 637001

Namakkal neurocare hospital

Address: 297/1 kasiyar street,paranathy road,,
Namakkal, 637001

Sabari Children's Hospital

Address: 31-B, Mohanur Road, Opp to Govt Boys
Higher Sec School (South), Namakkal, Tamil Nadu
637001
Phone: 04286 220 148

Chellam Hospital

Address: No. 4A, Dr.Sankaran Road, Near BSNL
Office, Thillaipuram, Namakkal, Tamil Nadu 637001
Phone: 04286 223 189

Dr. K. MURUGESAN , MBBS,AFIH.,

Nirmala Hospital

Address: Paramathi Rd, Thillaipuram, Namakkal,
Tamil Nadu 637001
Phone: 04286 220 044

Shanthi Hospitals

Address: No: 60/65, Rangar Sannathi Street, Near
Indian Bank, Tiruchengode - Namakkal - Trichy Rd,
Periyapatti, Tamil Nadu 637001

Saravana Hospital

Address: 89, Trichy Main Road, Ganesapuram,
Namakkal, Tamil Nadu 637001
Phone: 04286 222 150

Ganga Hospital

 Address: 637001, Natarajapuram, Kamaraj Nagar,
Namakkal, Tamil Nadu 637001

Phone: 04286 248 565

Sugam Childrens Hospital
Address: Tiruchengode - Namakkal - Trichy Rd,
Thillaipuram, Namakkal, Tamil Nadu 637001
Phone: 04286 222 532

Dr. K. MURUGESAN , MBBS,AFIH.,

12.ERODE

KMCH Speciality Hospital
Address: 16, Palaniappa Street, Landmark: Opp. to
GH, Erode, Tamil Nadu 638009
 Phone: 0424 225 6456

City Hospital

Address: 87, RKV Road, Opposite Krishna Theater,
Erode, Tamil Nadu 638003
Phone: 0424 221 4000

CK Hospital

Address: Kadar Moodein St, Kollampalayam, Erode,
Tamil Nadu 638001
Phone: 0424 226 9635

Care 24 Medical Center & Hospital

Address: 78/1to 10.Perundurai road, Near Parimalam
Mahal, behind Skoda Car Show room, Tamil Nadu
638012
Phone: 0424 266 6666

Erode Trust Hospital

Address: 42/14, Chinnamuthu Ii Street, Natersar Mill
Enclave, Perundurai Rd, Erode, Tamil Nadu 638001

Dr. K. MURUGESAN , MBBS,AFIH.,

Sudha Institute of Medical Sciences
Address: No.162 / 181, Perundurai Rd,
Edayankattuvalasu, Erode, Tamil Nadu 638011
Phone: 0424 245 4545

Lotus Hospital
Address: 90th Thayumanava Sundaram Street
Poondurai Main Road, Kollampalayam, Erode, Tamil
Nadu 638002
Phone: 0424 228 2828

TPN Hospitals
Address: 194, Perundurai Road, Veerapam Palayam
Pirivu, Near Honda showroom, Erode, Tamil Nadu
638011

Be Well Hospital
Address: 5&7, Gandhiji Rd, Surampattivalasu, Erode,
Tamil Nadu 638001

M R Hospital

Address: 246, Nethaji Rd, Marapalam, Erode, Tamil
Nadu 638001
Phone: 0424 225 6862

Kovai Medical Center

Address: 02/2, Gandhi Nagar, Colony, Perundurai Rd,
NGO Colony, Erode, Tamil Nadu 638011
Phone: 0424 226 2838

GEM Hospital

Address: 5, Muthukaruppannan Street, Gandhi
Nagar, Erode, Tamil Nadu 638009
Phone: 0424 403 1355

Ashwin Hospital

Address: SURAMPATTI NALL ROAD, 212/545, SKC
Road, Kaikolar Thottam, Chidambaram Colony,

Dr. K. MURUGESAN , MBBS,AFIH.,

Erode, Tamil Nadu 638001
Phone: 0424 225 8393

Nishant Hospital
Address: Near Vasan Eye Care Hospital, 279, EVN Rd,
Chidambaram Colony, Erode, Tamil Nadu 638009
Phone: 0424 225 7999

Thanthai Periyar Government Headquarters Hospital
Address: EVN Road, Erode, Tamil Nadu 638009
Phone: 0424 225 3676

Senthil Multi Speciality Hospital
Address: 547, Perundurai Rd, Edayankattuvalasu,
Erode, Tamil Nadu 638011
Phone: 0424 226 0377

Kumarasamy Hospital
Address: H 137, Periyar Nagar, Erode, Tamil Nadu
638011

Phone: 0424 225 7222

Thangam Hospital

Address: C Krishnasamy", H-123, Head Post Office
Backside, Periyar Nagar, Erode, Tamil Nadu 638001
Phone: 0424 225 9030

Bharani Paventhan Multispeciality Hospital

Address: Plot no 74,Sampath Nagar, Erode, Tamil
Nadu 638011

Baby Hospital

Address: 171, Nethaji road, Marappaalam, Erode,
Tamil Nadu 638001
Phone: 0424 226 1075

Erode Medical Center

Address: No.374/2, R.S, 3, & 5, Perundurai Rd, Erode,
Tamil Nadu 638011
Phone: 0424 288 8555

Dr. K. MURUGESAN , MBBS,AFIH.,

Kalyani Kidney Care Centre
Address: No. 104, Sampath Nagar Main Road, Near
to Kongu Kalaiyarangam, Sampath Nagar, Erode,
Tamil Nadu 638009
Phone: 0424 226 6949

Om Sakthi Hospital
Address: No.84, Poondurai Road, Telephone Nagar,
Moolapalayam Post Office, Chettipalayam, Erode,
Tamil Nadu 638002
Phone: 0424 228 1571

13.NILGIRIS

KMF Hospital

Address: Mission Compound, Kotagiri-The Nilgris,,

Dr. K. MURUGESAN , MBBS,AFIH.,

The Nilgris,, Tamil Nadu 643217
Phone: 04266 271 737

Nankem Hospital

Address: Near Y.W.C.A, Bedford, Coonoor, Tamil
Nadu 643101
Phone: 0423 223 1550

GTMO Hospital

Address: Nilgiris, NH-67, Nagapattinam Coimbatore
Gundlupet Highway, Gudalur, Gudalur, 643212
Phone: 04262 261 800

Vijaya Hospital

Address: Ettines Road, Ooty, Tamil Nadu 643001
Phone: 0423 244 2248

Sagayamatha Hospital

Address: Balaclava, Coonoor, Tamil Nadu 643102
Phone: 0423 220 6979

PSG Hospitals

Address: Avinash Road, Peelamedu, Coimbatore,
Tamil Nadu 643201
Phone: 0422 434 5260

Taj Hospital

Address: Gudalur, Tamil Nadu 643212
Phone: 04262 261 228

Pushpa hospital

Address: Coonoor-Kattabettu-Kotagiri Road,
Alwarpet, Coonoor, Tamil Nadu 643101

Sanhita Hospital

Address: Dasaprakash Rd, Bishop Down, Fern Hill,
Ooty, Tamil Nadu 643001
Phone: 0423 244 3671

Dr. K. MURUGESAN , MBBS,AFIH.,

S M Hospital

Address: 29/108, Coonoor Rd, Bombay Castel, Ooty,
Tamil Nadu 643001
Phone: 0423 244 2258

Pushpagiri Mission Hospital

Address: Gudalur, Tamil Nadu 643212

Mountain Top Clinic

Address: 3/245 B, Pannamadai Road, Hulical,
Niligirs,, Coonoor, Tamil Nadu 643234

Government Lawley Hospital

Address: NH 67, Vannarpet, Coonoor, Tamil Nadu
643101

Kotagiri Government Hospital

Address: Main Bazar Road, SH 15, Kotagiri, Tamil
Nadu 643217
Phone: 04266 271 309

14.ARIYALUR

MM Multi Speciality Hospital

Address: Rajajinagar, Ariyalur, Tamil Nadu 621704

Dr. K. MURUGESAN , MBBS,AFIH.,

Phone: 04329 222 433

RR Hospital

Address: Thandavarayan St, Ethraj Nagar, Ariyalur,
Tamil Nadu 621704
Phone: 04329 223 201

VGR hospital (eye,skin) speciality centre

Address: Komutty Theru, Ethraj Nagar, Ariyalur,
Tamil Nadu 621704
Phone: 04329 220 749

KMS HOAPITAL

Address: MIN Nagar, Ariyalur, Tamil Nadu 621704
Phone: 04329 222 199

A.S NURSING HOME

Address: Pattunoolkara Theru, Ethraj Nagar, Ariyalur,
Tamil Nadu 621704

Ariyalur Government Hospital

Address: Rajajinagar, Ariyalur, Tamil Nadu 621704
Phone: 04329 224 050

KVS Hospital

Address: Jayankondam Road, Valajanagaram,
Ariyalur, Tamil Nadu 621704

ARIYALUR GOLDEN HOSPITAL PVT LTD

Address: Ariyalur - Sendurai Road, Periyar Nagar,
Ariyalur, Tamil Nadu 621704

Dr. K. MURUGESAN , MBBS,AFIH.,

15.PERAMBALUR

Lakshmi Hospital

Address: No: 7A/44-1D, MG Puram, Rover School
Road, Perambalur, Tamil Nadu 621212

Phone: 04328 278 757

M.G.HOSPITAL

Address: Thuraimangalam, Perambalur, Tamil Nadu
621212

Siva Hospital

Address: 154, Venkatesapuram, Perambalur, Tamil
Nadu 621212
Phone: 04328 277 507

Arputhaa Medical Care Hospital

Address: 482 /2B, Venkatesapuram,Near New Bus
Stand,, SH 142, Perambalur, Tamil Nadu 621212
Phone: 04328 225 696

Annai Hospital

Address: opposite rajan petrol bunk, 106/f, Thuraiyur
- Perambalur Rd, Sungu Pettai, Perambalur, Tamil

Dr. K. MURUGESAN , MBBS,AFIH.,

Nadu 621212
Phone: 04328 225 825

Madhu Hospital

Address: Ariyalur Bypass Road, SH 142, M M Nagar,
Perambalur, 621220

Chellam Hospital

Address: Trichy Main Rd, Sungu Pettai, Perambalur,
Tamil Nadu 621212
Phone: 04328 277 570

Venkatesan Hospital

Address: 121,Venkatesapuram,Trichy Main Road,
Perambalur, Tamil Nadu 621212
Phone: 04328 224 500

Perambalur Goverment Head Quaters Hospital

Address: Thuraiyur - Perambalur Rd, Super Nagar,
Perambalur, Tamil Nadu 621212
Phone: 04328 277 128

Dhanalakshmi Srinivasan Hospital

Address: Sungu Pettai, Perambalur, Tamil Nadu 621212

SKS Hospital

Address: SH 142, Sungu Pettai, Perambalur, Tamil Nadu 621212

Dr. K. MURUGESAN , MBBS,AFIH.,

16.THIRUCHIRAPALLI

Kauvery Hospital
Address: No. 6, Royal Rd, Cantonment,
Tiruchirappalli, Tamil Nadu 620001
Phone: 0431 407 7777

GVN Hospital

Address: Near, 46 Ahmed Road, Super Bazaar,
Singarathope, Tiruchirappalli, Tamil Nadu 620008
Phone: 0431 270 0712

Apollo Hospital

Address: Serviced Apartment, Chennai Bypass Road
Near High Point, Ariyamangalam Area,
Tiruchirappalli, Tamil Nadu 620008
Phone: 0431 330 7777

Kauvery Hospital

Address: No.1, K.C.Road, Tennur, Tiruchirappalli,
Tamil Nadu 620017
Phone: 0431 402 2555

Dr. K. MURUGESAN , MBBS,AFIH.,

CSI Mission General Hospital
Address: Salai Road, Woraiur, Ramalinga Nagar,
Tiruchirappalli, Tamil Nadu 620003
Phone: 0431 276 1927

Dr. G. Viswanathan Speciality Hospitals
Address: Near Jaipur Bhavan Function Hall, No-25
A1/A2, Trichy Chennai Trunk Road, Tiruchirappalli,
Tamil Nadu 620005
Phone: 0431 403 1234

ABC Hospital
Address: 1, Annamalai Nagar Main Rd, Annamalai
Nagar, Woraiyur, Tiruchirappalli, Tamil Nadu 620018
Phone: 0431 407 7111

Retna Global Hospital (RGH)
Address: 95/1, Pattabiraman Salai, Anna Nagar,
Tennur, Tiruchirappalli, Tamil Nadu 620017

Frontline Hospitals
Address: 37 & 39, Near Anna Statue, Chinathamani

Bazzar, Tamil Nadu 620002
Phone: 0431 271 6666

Velan Speciality Hospitals

Address: No-1, Jail Corner, Highways Colony,
Subramaniyapuram, Tiruchirappalli, Tamil Nadu
620020
Phone: 0431 233 4444

Cethar hospitals

Address: No-C-108 Fort Station Road, 5th Cross Rd,
Thillai Nagar, Tiruchirappalli, Tamil Nadu 620018
Phone: 077080 68060

Nalam Hospital

Address: 158, Highway Colony, Sundarraj Nagar,
Subramaniyapuram, Tiruchirappalli, Tamil Nadu
620020
Phone: 0431 233 2695

Arul Hospital

Address: 6, T.V.K. Nagar, Opp Maruthi Hospital,

Dr. K. MURUGESAN , MBBS,AFIH.,

Vannarapettai, Puthur, Tiruchirappalli, Tamil Nadu
620017

Kauvery Heart City
Address: No-52, Alexandria Rd, Near Military
Canteen, Cantonment, Tiruchirappalli, Tamil Nadu
620001
Phone: 0431 400 3500

Maruti Hospital
Address: 95, Pattabiraman Salai, Anna Nagar,
Tennur, Tiruchirappalli, Tamil Nadu 620017
Phone: 0431 224 0000

Child Jesus Hospital
Address: Promenade Road, Opp TABS Complex,
Cantonment, Tiruchirappalli, Tamil Nadu 620001
Phone: 0431 241 0816

Trichy Diabetes Speciality Center

Address: C-87, Shastri Rd, North East Extension,
Thillai Nagar, Tiruchirappalli, Tamil Nadu 620017
Phone: 0431 274 2091

Mathuram Hospital

Address: 3a, 3b E.V.R Road Guru Medical Hall
Puthur(opp, Government Hospital, Tiruchirappalli,
Tamil Nadu 620017

Mahathma Eye Hospital

Address: No-6, Ramarao Agraharam, Srinivasapuram,
Sheshapuram, Tennur, Tiruchirappalli, Tamil Nadu
620017
Phone: 0431 274 0494

Olympia Hospital & Research Centre

Address: 47, 47-A, Puthur High Road, Puthur,
Tiruchirappalli, Tamil Nadu 620017

SVH Speciality Hospital

Address: NO.34, 6th Cross W, Thillai Nagar,
Tiruchirappalli, Tamil Nadu 620018

Dr. K. MURUGESAN , MBBS,AFIH.,

Phone: 0431 402 4770

Joseph Eye Hospital

Address: Nagapattinam - Coimbatore - Gundlupet
Hwy, Melapudur, Sangillyandapuram, Tiruchirappalli,
Tamil Nadu 620001
Phone: 0431 246 0622

Gitanjali Medical Centre

Address: 5, Allithurai Rd, Aruna Nagar, Puthur,
Bharathi Nagar, Tiruchirappalli, Tamil Nadu 620017
Phone: 0431 277 6600

Deepan Hospital

Address: No. 50, Bishop Rd, Puthur, Thillai Nagar,
Tiruchirappalli, Tamil Nadu 620017
Phone: 0431 279 2449

Tilak Hospitals

Address: 103 A/2 Devar colony, 1st Cross, Thillai
Nagar, Tiruchirappalli, Tamil Nadu 620018
Phone: 0431 276 2288

Mahatma Gandhi Memorial Government Hospital

Address: Bharthi Nagar, Puthur, Thillai Nagar,
Tiruchirappalli, Tamil Nadu 620017
Phone: 0431 277 1465

Janet Nursing Home

Address: 21B, Officers Colony Road,
Venganadapuram, Puthur, Opp Fish Market,
Tiruchirappalli, Tamil Nadu 620017
Phone: 0431 279 2543

Ananthagiri Hospital

Address: C-1, 1st Cross Rd, North East Extension,
Thillai Nagar, Tiruchirappalli, Tamil Nadu 620018

Ayesha Hospital

Address: Rahumaniya Puram, Thillai Nagar,
Tiruchirappalli, Tamil Nadu 620018
Phone: 0431 454 2277

Krishna Hospital

Address: 1, KK Nagar Main Rd, Krishna Moorthy
Nagar, K.K Nagar, Tiruchirappalli, Tamil Nadu 620021

Dr. K. MURUGESAN , MBBS,AFIH.,

Phone: 0431 245 5886

17. KARUR

Apollo Hospital
Address: 163 A- E, Allwyn Nagar, 30, LGB Nagar,
Kovai Main Rd, Vaiyapuri Nagar, Ramanujam Nagar,
Karur, Tamil Nadu 639002

Amaravathi Hospital

Address: 74, Ramanujam Nagar, Karur, Tamil Nadu
639002

Aarthy Eye Hospital

Address: 16 (62) Sengunthapuram Main Road,
Railway Road, Karur, Tamil Nadu 639002
Phone: 04324 233 163

Gugan Hospital

Address: Anna Nagar, Karur, Tamil Nadu 639001
Phone: 04324 241 068

Abs hospital

Address: No 161 B/5 North, Siva Sakthi Nagar,
Thanthonimalai, Karur, Tamil Nadu 639005
Phone: 04324 255 300

Nirmala Hospital

Dr. K. MURUGESAN , MBBS,AFIH.,

Address: Ramakrishnapuram, Karur, Tamil Nadu
639001

E.R.S Hospital

Address: North Pradhaksanam Road,
Ramakrishnapuram, Karur, Tamil Nadu 639001

Abirami Maternity Centre

Address: 27, Narasimapuram South, Covai Road,
Covai Road, Karur, Tamil Nadu 639001
Phone: 04324 261 165

Priyanka Hospital

Address: 39, Pradarshanam Road,
Ramakrishnapuram, Karur, Tamil Nadu 639001

Vidiyal Hospital

Address: Ram nagar,Karur trichy main road,
Gandhigramam, Karur, Tamil Nadu 613004
Phone: 04324 242 552

Nesi Eye Care Hospital
Address: Gandhi Puram, Karur, Tamil Nadu 639002
Phone: 04324 234 599

Sri anjana nursing home
Address: No. 7/1 South Narasimmapram, Light House
Corner, SH74, Karur, Tamil Nadu 639001
Phone: 04324 261 878

Raj Ortho Hospital
Address: TVK Road, Gowripuram, Karur, Tamil Nadu
639001

Preetha Hospital
Address: Kamarajapuram, Karur, Tamil Nadu 639002

Dr. K. MURUGESAN , MBBS,AFIH.,

18.THIRUPPUR

Sri Kumaran Hospital
Address: 774, P. N. Road, Near New Bus Stand, Postal
Colony, Tiruppur, Tamil Nadu 641602
Phone: 0421 247 8787

Revathi Medical Center

Address: No 10, Valayangadu Main Rd, Valagan,
Kumar Nagar, Tiruppur, Tamil Nadu 641603
Phone: 0421 433 2211

TMF Hospital

Address: Number 1, Kannipiran Colony,
Sabapathipuram, Tiruppur, Tamil Nadu 641601
Phone: 0421 220 3657

Sree Saran Medical Centre

Address: P.N.Road, Poyampalayam Bus stop,
Tiruppur, Tamil Nadu 641602
Phone: 0421 248 5455

Deepa Hospital

Dr. K. MURUGESAN , MBBS,AFIH.,

Address: 2nd St Stanes Rd, KNP Puram, Odakkadu,
Tiruppur, Tamil Nadu 641687
Phone: 0421 224 2225

AMC Super Speciality Hospital

Address: 141, Kamaraj Road, Palladam Main Road,
Tiruppur, Tamil Nadu 641604

AG Hospital

Address: No 34, Kpn Colony Main Road , 3rd Street,
Near Nalini Hospital, Tiruppur, Tamil Nadu 641602
Phone: 0421 220 2444

Bala Ortho Hospital

Address: Opposite Govt Hospital, Near Bharath
Petrol Bunk, Dharapuram Road, Tiruppur, Tamil
Nadu 641605
Phone: 0421 432 2226

Rams Hospital

Address: No. 82, Murungappalayam Main Road
Murugappalayam Extension, Opp. Bharat Petrol

Bunk, Murungapalayam, Kumar Nagar, Tiruppur,
Tamil Nadu 641603
Phone: 0421 220 0456

Lifeguard hospital

Address: Tiruppur - Palladam Rd, Sheriff Colony
Extension, Tiruppur, Tamil Nadu 641604

Gem Hospital

Address: Kumarnathapuram, Tiruppur, Tamil Nadu
641603
Phone: 0421 432 5678

City Ortho Hospital

Address: 7, 60 Feet Rd, Kumarnathapuram, Tiruppur,
Tamil Nadu 641602
Phone: 0421 247 4999

OMS Hospital

Address: 4/490A, Palladam Road, Bharathi Nagar,
Veerapandi, Tiruppur, Tamil Nadu 641605
Phone: 0421 424 6444

Dr. K. MURUGESAN , MBBS,AFIH.,

Malar Priya Medical Center

Address: 1946-M,Ponnamal Nagar, Pandian Nagar,
Tiruppur, Tamil Nadu 641602

Kongu Heart Center Hospital

Address: No. 80, Dharapuram Rd, Karattankadu Bus
Stop, K N P Colony, Karattangkadu, Tiruppur, Tamil
Nadu 641608

19 . COIMBATORE

Ganga Hospital
Address: No. 313, Mettupalayam Road, Saibaba Koil,
Coimbatore, Tamil Nadu 641043
Phone: 0422 248 5000

Dr. K. MURUGESAN , MBBS,AFIH.,

PSG Hospitals

Address: Masakalipalayam, Peelamedu, Coimbatore, Tamil Nadu 641004
Phone: 0422 257 0170

KG Hospital

Address: 5, Government Arts College Rd, Opposite Court, Gopalapuram, Coimbatore, Tamil Nadu 641018
Phone: 0422 221 2121

Kovai Medical Center and Hospital

Address: 99, Avinashi Rd, TNHB Colony, Indira Nagar, Civil Aerodrome Post, Peelamedu, Coimbatore, Tamil Nadu 641014
Phone: 0422 432 3800

SPT Hospitals

Address: 50, Vivekananda Rd, Peranaidu Layout, Ram
Nagar, Coimbatore, Tamil Nadu 641009
Phone: 0422 223 2525

Sree Abirami Hospital Private Limited
Address: No. 33, Madukkarai Main Rd,
Sundarapuram, Kurichi, Coimbatore, Tamil Nadu
641024
Phone: 0422 246 6666

KMCH City Center Hospital
Address: No.18, Vivekananda Road, Ram Nagar,
Coimbatore, Tamil Nadu 641009
Phone: 0422 437 8720

G. Kuppuswamy Naidu Memorial Hospital
Address: Netaji Rd, P N Palayam, Coimbatore, Tamil
Nadu 641037
Phone: 0422 224 5000

VG Hospital

Dr. K. MURUGESAN , MBBS,AFIH.,

Address: 76/A, Mettupalayam Rd, VKL Nagar,
Thudiyalur, Coimbatore, Tamil Nadu 641034
Phone: 0422 264 2071

Rex Ortho Hospital

Address: Bus Stop, 43, Shanmugam Rd, RR Layout,
R.S. Puram, Coimbatore, Tamil Nadu 641002
Phone: 0422 254 2542

Shree Hospital

Address: 718, Trichy Rd, Dhamu Nagar, Puliakulam,
Coimbatore, Tamil Nadu 641045
Phone: 0422 231 8311

GEM Hospital And Research Center

Address: 45, Pankaja Mills Rd, Palaniappa Nagar,
Sowripalayam Pirivu, Ramanathapuram, Coimbatore,
Tamil Nadu 641045
Phone: 0422 232 5100

Sheela Hospital

Address: 117, E Power House Rd, Tatabad,
Coimbatore, Tamil Nadu 641012
Phone: 0422 249 8381

Coimbatore Kidney Centre Multi Speciality Hospital

Address: No. 738 - B, Puliakulam Road, Near Lakshmi
Mills, Coimbatore, Tamil Nadu 641045
Phone: 0422 231 2006

Sumith Hospital

Address: Vilankurichi Rd, Opp GRG Ground, Hope
College, Peelamedu, Coimbatore, Tamil Nadu
641004
Phone: 0422 457 2222

NG Hospital And Research Centre

Address: 577 Trichy Road Near B-5 Police Station,
Singanallur, Coimbatore, Tamil Nadu 641005
Phone: 0422 259 5963

Dr. K. MURUGESAN , MBBS,AFIH.,

20 .NAGAPATTINAM

Ansari Hospital
Address: Naganathar Sannathi, Melakottaivasal,
Nagore, Nagapattinam, Tamil Nadu

Phone: 04365 224 527

Nagai Hospital

Address: Opp. Mangala Mahal, Puthur, Manjakkollai,
Nagapattinam, Tamil Nadu 611106
Phone: 04365 224 650

Sri Venkateswara Hospital

Address: Naduvar Sannathi, Nagapattinam, East
Coast Road, Nagapattinam, Nagapattinam, 611001
Phone: 04365 225 925

Nagapattinam Government Headquarters Hospital

Address: Elancheran Nagar, Nagapattinam, Tamil
Nadu 611001
Phone: 04365 242 459

Sakthi Balan Hospital

Dr. K. MURUGESAN , MBBS,AFIH.,

Address: Coimbatore Nagapattinam Highway, Kizh
Velur, Tamil Nadu 611104
Phone: 04365 275 545

21.TANJAVUR

Anu Hospital
Address: No.69, Trichy Road, LMR : Convent,
Thanjavur, Tamil Nadu 613007
Phone: 04362 275 092

Meenakshi Hospital

Address: 244/2, Trichy Main Road, Near New Bus
Stand, Nilagiri Therkku Thottam, Thanjavur, Tamil
Nadu 613005
Phone: 04362 226 474

MR Hospitals

Address: 1, Pudukottai Road, Yagappa Nagar,
Thanjavur, Tamil Nadu 613007
Phone: 04362 278 005

Sivapreethi Hospital

Address: 33-35, S.Natrajan Nagar, Pudukkottai Road,
Thanjavur, Tamil Nadu 613005
Phone: 04362 226 376

Dr. K. MURUGESAN , MBBS,AFIH.,

Vinodhagan Memorial Hospital (P) Ltd
Address: No.3120 & 3121, Trichy Road, Thanjavur,
Tamil Nadu 613007
Phone: 04362 234 884

NM Hospital Pvt Ltd
Address: Plot No: 3275, 1/a-1, Ramakrishnapuram,
Opp to Manimandabam, Thanjavur, Tamil Nadu
613007
Phone: 04362 237 006

KG Multi Speciality Hospital And Research Centre
Address: 2nd Street, VOC Nagar, Parisutham Nagar,
Thanjavur, Tamil Nadu 613007
Phone: 04362 239 919

Royal Hospital
Address: 1624, South Main Street, Near Singaram
Medicals, Thanjavur, Tamil Nadu 613009
Phone: 04362 238 989

S.B. Hospital Urology, Nephrology & Fertility

Research Centre
Address: Medical College Road, Rajappa Nagar,
Thanjavur, Tamil Nadu 613007
Phone: 04362 236 872

Keerthana Hospital

Address: 51, GA Canal Rd, Attar Mohalla, Thanjavur,
Tamil Nadu 613001
Phone: 04362 279 827

AKC Hospital

Address: No.26, Shivaji Nagar, Oppo. Adlabs Theatre,
Tamil Nadu 613001
Phone: 04362 230 136

KDR Hospital

Address: 1 & 2, VNS Garden, Ramakrishnapuram,
Arulananda Nagar West Extension, Thanjavur, Tamil
Nadu 613007
Phone: 04362 230 379

G.M Hospital

Address: Membalam, No.3 Selvam Naga, Thanjavur,

Dr. K. MURUGESAN , MBBS,AFIH.,

Tamil Nadu 613007
Phone: 04362 231 134

MG Hospitals

Address: 16, Rajarajan Nagar 1st St, Arulananda
Nagar, Philomina Nagar, Thanjavur, Tamil Nadu
613007
Phone: 04362 234 142

Apex Heart Hospital

Address: Bus Stop, 9A, Selvam Nagar, Medical
College Road, Near Ganapathy Nagar, Thanjavur,
Tamil Nadu 613007
Phone: 04362 273 322

Vinothagan Hospital

Address: State Highway 99A, Parisutham Nagar,
Thanjavur, Tamil Nadu 613007
Phone: 04362 234 885

Krishna childcare centre

Address: VNS Garden, Parisutham Nagar, Thanjavur,
Tamil Nadu 613007

Government Raja Mirasudar Hospital
Address: Hospital Rd, Attar Mohalla, Thanjavur, Tamil
Nadu 613001

Dr A P J Abdul Kalam Centre for Oncology-Meenakshi Hospital
Address: Meenakshi Hospital, 244/2, Trichy Main
Road, Near Bus Stand, Nilagiri Therkku Thottam,
New, New Housing Unit, Thanjavur, Tamil Nadu
613005

Gowri Sankar Kidney Care Centre
Address: Mary's Arcade, First Floor, Near Our lady
Hospital, Arulananda Nagar West Extension,
Thanjavur, Tamil Nadu 613007

Dr. K. MURUGESAN , MBBS,AFIH.,

Phone: 04362 278 909

22. THIRUVARUR

Lakshana Hospitals
Address: SH 65, Madapuram, Thiruvarur, Tamil Nadu
610001

Phone: 04366 240 21

TMC Hospital TIRUVARUR MEDICAL CENTRE (P) LTD
Address: Near temple tank, Javulikkara Street,
Thiruvarur, Tamil Nadu 610001
Phone: 04366 242 292

Venkateshwara Hospitals
Address: Swamy Mada St, Madapuram, Thiruvarur,
Tamil Nadu 610001

Parvathi Hospitals
Address: SH 65, Madapuram, Thiruvarur, Tamil Nadu
610001
Phone: 04366 242 236

Dr. K. MURUGESAN , MBBS,AFIH.,

Navajeevan Multi Speciality Hospital
Address: No: 3/4B, Thanjai Salai, Near TNCSC
Godown & Collector Office, Vilamal, Thiruvarur,
Tamil Nadu 610004

23. PUDUKKOTTAI

Muthu Meenakshi Hospitals Pvt Ltd

Address: South 4th Street, Near Anna Statue,
Marthandapuram, Pudukkottai, Tamil Nadu 622001
Phone: 04322 242 424

Be Well Hospital

Address: 5, 5371, Alangudi Rd, Pudukkottai, Tamil
Nadu 622001

TEAM Hospital

Address: Near, Keeranur Bus Stand Rd,
Santhanathapuram, Pudukkottai, Tamil Nadu 622001
Phone: 04322 228 866

Shree Meenakshi Multispeciality Hospital

Address: 4215 South 4th street, 4215 South 4th
Street
Phone: 04322 220 234

SK Hospital

Dr. K. MURUGESAN , MBBS,AFIH.,

Address: Puda Nagar, Pudukkottai, NH-226,
Thanjavur Gandharvakottai Pudukkottai Road,
Pudukkottai, Pudukkottai, 622001
Phone: 04322 270 055

24.DINDIGAL

JCB Hospitals

Address: No.1, VEEPPAANTHOPPU STREET, Palani
Road, Dindigul, Tamil Nadu 624001

Phone: 0451 243 3993

Dharshini Hospitals

Address: 34, Narayana Nagar, Dindigul, Tamil Nadu 624001

Raksha Hospital

Address: 80 Feet Road, Nehruji Nagar, Dindigul, Tamil Nadu 624001
Phone: 0451 270 0700

Best Hospital

Address: 90/1, vivekanada nagar, Trichy - Dindugal Rd, Anna Nagar, Dindigul, Tamil Nadu 624001
Phone: 0451 242 9240

Shifa Hospital and Fertility Centre

Address: Chennamanayakkanpatty Main Road, Near

Dr. K. MURUGESAN , MBBS,AFIH.,

Collector's Office, Dindigul, Tamil Nadu 624004

JJ Arul Hospital
Address: Telephone colony road, Karunanidhi Nagar,
Dindigul, Tamil Nadu 624001
Phone: 0451 242 5454

Raja Rajeshwari Nursing Home
Address: 46, Spencer Compound, Dindigul, Tamil
Nadu 624001
Phone: 0451 242 2442

25 .SIVAGANGAI

Government Sivagangai Medical College and Hospital

Address: Manamadurai road, Sivagangai, Sivaganga, Tamil Nadu 630562

Dr. K. MURUGESAN , MBBS,AFIH.,

Phone: 04575 243 344

Karthick Hospitals
Address: 96, SH 33, Aranmanai Vaasal, Sivaganga,
Tamil Nadu 630561
Phone: 04575 241 604

Sabari maternity and children hospital
Address: 4/106 sabari hospital lane justice
rajasekaran street. sivagangai630561
Phone: 04575 245 431

Vasan Eye Care Hospital
Address: Gowri Vilasam, Marakadai Bus Stop,Old
Palace, Sivagangai, Sivaganga, Tamil Nadu 630561
Phone: 04575 398 900

Apollo Reach Hospital

Address: Madurai Main Road, Managiri, Sivagangai
District, Karaikudi, Tamil Nadu 630307
Phone: 04565 223 700

Vikram Multispeciality Hospital

Address: 3/424, Ring Road Junction, Near Pandi
Kovil, Madurai Sivagangai Main Rd, Madurai, Tamil
Nadu 625020

Golden Hospital

Address: No.2/183/2, Sivagangai Main Rd,
Gomathipuram, Madurai, Tamil Nadu 625020
Phone: 0452 439 6975

Dr. K. MURUGESAN , MBBS,AFIH.,

26. MADURAI

Vadamalayan Hospitals
Address: 9A, Vallabh Bhai Road, 15/1,Jawahar Road,
Chockikulam, Madurai, Tamil Nadu 625002

Phone: 0452 254 5400

Apollo Speciality Hospitals

Address: 80 Feet Road, KK Nagar, Madurai, Tamil
Nadu 625020
Phone: 0452 258 0892

Meenakshi Mission Hospital & Research Centre

Address: Lake Area, melur Road, Near Mattuthavani
Bus Stand, Madurai, Tamil Nadu 625107
Phone: 0452 426 3000

BGM Hospital

Address: 249, Vishwanathapuram, New Natham
Connection Road, Iyer Bungalow, Madurai, Tamil
Nadu 625014
Phone: 0452 426 8211

Dr. K. MURUGESAN , MBBS,AFIH.,

NTC Hospitals

Address: No: 187, Thathaneri Main Road, Near ESI
Hospital, Vaithiyanathapuram, Madurai, Tamil Nadu
625018
Phone: 0452 266 0064

Devadoss Multispeciality Hospital

Address: 75, 1, Alagar Kovil Main Rd, Surveyor
Colony, K.Pudur, Madurai, Tamil Nadu 625007
Phone: 0452 452 1000

Velammal Medical College Hospital & Research Institute

Address: Madurai-Tuticorin Ring Road, Velammal,
Anuppanadi, Near Chinthamani Toll Gate, Madurai,
Tamil Nadu 625009
Phone: 0452 711 3333

Keerthi Hospitals

Address: Dinamalar Ave, Chokkalinga Nagar,
Ponmeni, Madurai, Tamil Nadu 625016
Phone: 0452 435 2121

Lakshmana Multispeciality Hospital

Address: 23, Tirupparankunram Road, Pykara,
Madurai, Tamil Nadu 625004
Phone: 0452 237 1369

Apollo First Med Hospitals

Address: No.484-B, West First Street, Near District
Court, K.K. Nagar, Madurai, Tamil Nadu 625020
Phone: 0452 252 5811

Vikram Multispeciality Hospital

Address: 3/424, Ring Road Junction, Near Pandi
Kovil, Madurai Sivagangai Main Rd, Madurai, Tamil
Nadu 625020

Dr. K. MURUGESAN , MBBS,AFIH.,

27.THENI

Nalam Hospital & Academy

Address: 63/2, Lake Road, Sri Ram Nagar, Theni,
Tamil Nadu 625531
Phone: 04546 253 777

Krishnammal Memorial Hospital

Address: No. 14, Periyakulam - Cumbum Road, Kottai
Kalam, Theni, Tamil Nadu 625531
Phone: 04546 250 700

NRT Hospital

Address: Madurai Main Rd, NRT Nagar, Theni, Tamil
Nadu 625531

Gayathri Medical Centre (P) Ltd

Address: 356, North Main Road, Aranmanai Pudhur,
Theni, Tamil Nadu 625531
Phone: 04546 253 770

Holy Redeemer Hospital

Dr. K. MURUGESAN , MBBS,AFIH.,

Address: Bathra Kaliyamman, Konduraja Line, Theni
Allinagaram, 625531
Phone: 04546 252 502

Udaya Nursing Home
Address: Periyakulam Road, Opp. Aravind Eye
Hospital, Sri Ram Nagar, Theni, Tamil Nadu 625531
Phone: 04546 262 303

28.RAMANATHAPURAM

A.R. Hospital

Dr. K. MURUGESAN , MBBS,AFIH.,

Address: Kochi - Madurai - Dhanushkodi Road,
Davendrar Nagar, Periyar Nagar, Ramanathapuram,
Tamil Nadu 623501
Phone: 04567 222 472

Pioneer Hospitals Pvt. Ltd

Address: No. 68, Madurai Road, Gobilthankavelu,
Ramanathapuram, Tamil Nadu 623501
Phone: 04567 221 317

Government Hospital

Address: National Highway 49, Chalai Bazar,
Ramanathapuram, Tamil Nadu 623501

Aasi multi speciality hospital

Address: No:6/1155-1,D'block opp to RTO
office,Rameswaram Road,Ramanathapuram.

Syed Ammal Trust Hospital

Address: No. 127, Swami Vivekananthar, Salai Street,
Ramanathapuram, Tamil Nadu 623501

Phone: 04567 220 312

Shifan Hospital

Address: NH 210, Chalai Bazar, Ramanathapuram,
Tamil Nadu 623501
Phone: 04567 221 453

Arogya Hospital

Address: Kenikarai, Ramanathapuram, Tamil Nadu
62350
Phone: 04567 222 888

JK Hospitals

Address: Bharathi Nagar, Ramanathapuram, Tamil
Nadu 623503
Phone: 04567 230 455

District Headquarters Hospital

Address: GH Rd, Chalai Bazar, Ramanathapuram,
Tamil Nadu 623501

Dr. K. MURUGESAN , MBBS,AFIH.,

Phone: 04567 220 309

29.VIRUDHUNAGAR

Lysander Hospital
Address: 142, W Car St, Sivagami Puram,
Virudhunagar, Tamil Nadu 626001
Phone: 04562 243 233

Thiruvengdam Hospital

Address: No: 66-T-1, Ramamoorthy Road, Near GH,
Virudhunagar, Tamil Nadu 626001
Phone: 04562 242 565

Dr. Muthusamy Hospital

Address: 20, 1, Link Rd, Professors colony, Anna
Nagar, Virudhunagar, Tamil Nadu 626001
Phone: 04562 265 222

Care AKPS Hospital

Address: 4A/4, Kasturibai Rd, Professors colony,
Anna Nagar, Virudhunagar, Tamil Nadu 626001
Phone: 04562 422 911

Shivashankar Hospital & Research Center

Address: 91/1A, Pullalakottai Rd, Sivagami Puram,

Dr. K. MURUGESAN , MBBS,AFIH.,

Virudhunagar, Tamil Nadu 626001
Phone: 04562 244 920

Government Hospital

Address: Ramamoorthy Rd, Professors colony, Anna
Nagar, Virudhunagar, Tamil Nadu 626001
Phone: 04562 243 880

MPNC Hospital

Address: ACG Multipurpose Stadium, Compost Rd,
Hanumaan Nagar, Virudhunagar, Tamil Nadu 626001
Phone: 04562 280 370

Chidambaram Nagammal Hospital

Address: 82/1, Aruppukottai Rd, Sivagami Puram,
Virudhunagar, Tamil Nadu 626001
Phone: 04562 280 570

Dr Jeevarajan Hospital

Address: Service Rd, GT Nagar, Virudhunagar, Tamil
Nadu 626001

VVV Hospital

Address: Service Rd, N.G.O Nagar, Chatrareddiapatti, Virudhunagar, Tamil Nadu 626001
Phone: 04562 266 540

Dr.Kalidoss Hospital

Address: 27/2 mathu naickenpatti road, Allampatti, Tamil Nadu 626001

Dr. K. MURUGESAN , MBBS,AFIH.,

30.THOOTHUKUDI

Rajesh Tilak Hospital
Address: 107J/79/53/1, 2, 3, P.C Road West,,
Millerpuram, Thoothukudi, Tamil Nadu 628008
Phone: 0461 233 3536

Sacred Heart Hospital

Address: Kandhasamy Puram, Thoothukudi, Tamil
Nadu 628002
Phone: 0461 236 0714

AVM Hospital

Address: No. 135, Palayamkottai Road, PSP Nagar,
Thoothukudi, Tamil Nadu 628003
Phone: 0461 232 5461

City Hospital

Address: 106, G/8, Palayamkottai Road, Millerpuram,
Thoothukudi, Tamil Nadu 628008

Dr. K. MURUGESAN , MBBS,AFIH.,

Sundaram Arulraj Hospitals
Address: 145/5B, Jeyaraj Road, Thoothukudi, Tamil
Nadu 628002
Phone: 0461 232 7661

Dheiva Nursing Home
Address: No: 209-A DMNS School Main Road
Opposite to, Dhamodhara Nagar, Thoothukudi, Tamil
Nadu 628002

Veeramani Hospital
Address: Opp. Subbiah Vidyalayam school, 1B/2,
Perumalpuram Rd, Pudugramam, Thoothukudi, Tamil
Nadu 628003
Phone: 0461 232 9682

31.THIRUNELVELI

Shifa Hospital
Address: 82, Near Junction Flyover, Kailasapuram,
Middle Street, Tirunelveli Town, Meenakshipuram,
Tirunelveli, Tamil Nadu 627001

Dr. K. MURUGESAN , MBBS,AFIH.,

Phone: 0462 232 3041

Rosemary Mission Hospitals

Address: 10/3, S Bypass Rd, Vannarpettai, Tirunelveli,
Tamil Nadu 627009
Phone: 0462 250 2211

Lakshmi Hospital

Address: 101-A, Madhurai Road, Udeyarpatti,
Tirunelveli, Tamil Nadu 627001
Phone: 0462 233 3830

Muthamil hospital

Address: No. 59, Trivandrum Road, Palayamkottai,
Tirunelveli, Tamil Nadu 627002
Phone: 0462 256 0783

Kani Hospitals

Address: 80, Cheranmahadevi Rd,, Pettai, Tirunelveli,
Tamil Nadu 627004
Phone: 0462 234 2612

Shree Sudharson Platinum Hospital

Address: 4/A, Salai Street, Vannarpettai, Tirunelveli,
Tamil Nadu 627003
Phone: 0462 250 1791

Tirunelveli Medical College

Address: High Ground Rd, Palayamkottai, Tirunelveli,
Tamil Nadu 627011
Phone: 0462 257 2733

CSI Jayaraj Annapackiam Mission Hospital

Address: 1B/2, North High Ground Road,
Palayamkottai, Tirunelveli, Tamil Nadu 627002
Phone: 0462 256 0194

Santhosh Hospital

Address: thachanallor,Thirunelveli, Thachanallur,
Tirunelveli, Tamil Nadu 627359

Royal hospital

Address: no:2,sharon street,ngo a colony,near stc college, 627007
Phone: 0462 255 4237

Annai Velankanni Multispeciality Hospital

Address: 1/111, Somasinayanar Street, Murugankurichi, Palayamkottai, Tirunelveli, Tamil Nadu 627002
Phone: 0462 250 1661

CSI Bell Pins Indrani Chelladurai Mission Hospital

Address: Samathanapuram Road, Palayamkottai, Tirunelveli, Tamil Nadu 627002
Phone: 0462 257 9811

Kartheek Nursing home

Address: S T C College Road, Perumalpuram, Tirunelveli, Tamil Nadu 627007

Phone: 0462 253 3724

Royal Children Hospital
Address: Royal Children Hospital, 2nd Sharon Street,
Kamarajar Rd, Tirunelveli, Tamil Nadu 627007
Phone: 0462 255 4237

Dr. K. MURUGESAN , MBBS,AFIH.,

32.KANYAKUMARI

Subam Speciality Hospital
Address: No. 215, Asambu Road, Opp. Smrv School,
Vadasery, Kanyakumari, Tamil Nadu 629001

Phone: 04652 272 146

CSI Hospital

Address: Neyyoor, Kanyakumari, SH-180, Colachel
Thiruvattar Road, Kanyakumari, Kanyakumari,
629802

Dr. Jeyasekharan Hospital

Address: Kottar-Parvathipuram Rd, Weavers Colony,
Nagercoil, Tamil Nadu 629003
Phone: 04652 230 019

Idroos Hospital

Address: Thittuvilai, Kanyakumari, SH-45,
Aralvaimozhi Nedumangadu Road, Kanyakumari,
Kanyakumari, 629852
Phone: 04652 281 786

Dr. K. MURUGESAN , MBBS,AFIH.,

Kanyakumari Medical Mission

Address: SH 180, Neyyoor, Tamil Nadu 629802

Phone: 04651 222 222

Jaya Hospital

Address: Arasamoodu, Pechiparai, Kanyakumari,

SH-90, Marthandam Pechiparai Road, Kanyakumari,

Kanyakumari, 629101

Phone: 04651 277 313

Krishna Kumar Orthopaedic Hospital

Address: Over Bridge, Parvathipuram, Nagercoil, K.K

DIST, Chunkan Kadai, Tamil Nadu 629003

Phone: 04652 231 322

Dr.Gopala Pillai's Hospital

Address: K .P Road, Ramavarmapuram, Simon Nagar,

Nagercoil, Tamil Nadu 629001

Phone: 04652 225 010

Dr. Jayaharan Memorial Hospital

Address: Court Road, 15/16-33, Victoria Press Rd,
Nagercoil, Tamil Nadu 629001
Phone: 04652 222 664

Holy Cross Hospital

Address: Pleasant Nagar, Nagercoil, Tamil Nadu
629001
Phone: 04652 230 897

Lister Hospital

Address: Main Road, Marthandam, Kanniyakumari
District, Nagercoil, Tamil Nadu 629165
Phone: 04652 225 152

Bensam Hospital

Address: Ms Road, NH 66 Near Kaliankadu Church,
Nagercoil, Tamil Nadu 629003
Phone: 04652 232 532

Dr. K. MURUGESAN , MBBS,AFIH.,

ABOUT THE AUTHOR

My name is Dr . K .Murugesan . I am A doctor . I have completed MBBS and AFIH . Contact me to give updates about your hospitals in your are which will be published in the next edition .my mail id is : doctor_india@hotmail.com

DISCLAIMER :

The information provided within this book is for general informational purposes only. While we try to keep the information up-to-date and correct, there are no representations or warranties, express or implied, about the completeness, accuracy, reliability, suitability or availability with respect to the information, products, services, or related graphics contained in this book for any purpose. Any use of this information is at your own risk. We do not recommend any hospital for your disease condition.Your family doctor will be a better adviser for chosing best hospital for your disease nature .

Dr. K. MURUGESAN , MBBS,AFIH.,

Dr. K. MURUGESAN , MBBS,AFIH.,

Dr. K. MURUGESAN , MBBS,AFIH.,

Dr. K. MURUGESAN , MBBS,AFIH.,